THE INSIDER'S GUIDE TO FISHING
CATFISH FISHING
LIKE A PRO

MARIE ROESSER

Published in 2024 by The Rosen Publishing Group, Inc.
2544 Clinton Street, Buffalo, NY 14224

Copyright © 2024 by The Rosen Publishing Group, Inc.

Portions of this work were originally authored by Robert Z. Cohen and published as *Catfish Fishing*. All new material in this edition was authored by Marie Roesser.

Editor: Therese M. Shea
Designer: Michael Flynn

All rights reserved. No part of this book may be reproduced in any form without permission in writing from the publisher, except by a reviewer.

Library of Congress Cataloging-in-Publication Data

Names: Roesser, Marie, author.
Title: Catfish fishing like a pro / Marie Roesser.
Description: Buffalo : Rosen Publishing, [2024] | Series: The insider's guide to fishing | Includes index.
Identifiers: LCCN 2023030800 | ISBN 9781499475951 (library binding) | ISBN 9781499475944 (paperback) | ISBN 9781499475968 (ebook)
Subjects: LCSH: Catfishing--Juvenile literature.
Classification: LCC SH691.C35 R64 2024 | DDC 799.17/492--dc23/eng/20230711
LC record available at https://lccn.loc.gov/2023030800

Some of the images in this book illustrate individuals who are models. The depictions do not imply actual situations or events.

Manufactured in the United States of America

CPSIA Compliance Information: Batch #CWRYA24. For further information, contact Rosen Publishing at 1-800-237-9932.

CONTENTS

INTRODUCTION 4

CHAPTER 1
BE PREPARED 8

CHAPTER 2
GET TO KNOW THE CATFISH 22

CHAPTER 3
TACKLE AND TECHNIQUE 38

CHAPTER 4
CAUGHT IT! NOW WHAT? 50

CHAPTER 5
CATFISH AND NATURE 62

GLOSSARY 74
FOR FURTHER READING 75
FOR MORE INFORMATION 76
INDEX 78
ABOUT THE AUTHOR/CONSULTANT 80

INTRODUCTION

Wherever you live, you likely live near a freshwater pond, lake, river, or stream where catfish lurk under the surface. That makes catfish some of the most accessible game fish, or fish caught for sport, in North America. You don't need a fancy, expensive rod and reel to catch these fish. Nearly any fishing rod will do, though you'll want something a bit stronger for larger catfish. Some people even catch catfish with a handline, which is just some fishing line, hooks, and bait. And others "noodle," or catch them with their hands! But this book is mostly about rod-and-reel fishing. Whether you're hoping to catch a catfish to eat or just pursuing the thrill of a catch and release, get ready to become a catfish—and catfishing—expert.

Catfish might not be the most attractive fish under the surface. They're sort of odd looking with a flattened head and those "whiskers," called barbels, on their chin and on the sides of their mouth. But these make them easy to recognize. They also give them their name, as they look like a cat's whiskers. And, some say, these fish make a purring noise when taken from the water! Catfish are some of the tastiest fish out there, especially the ones that live in clean waters. That's why catfish are often featured on menus in seafood restaurants and in cookbooks, particularly those about southern U.S. cuisine. They're a fish that many people around the world like to eat.

Catfish fishing is a sport that anyone can try. Many experienced people who fish enjoy chasing the "big cats"!

Because catfish are widespread and tasty, catching them is a popular kind of sport fishing. They're not necessarily the easiest fish to bring in, however! In fact, with catfish, you need to be prepared for anything. You may think you're fishing for a small bullhead catfish and end up with a whopper of a flathead catfish. Some anglers report struggling with a large catch for nearly an hour. Most are happy to do it for the fun photo opportunity and the possibility of scoring a record catch.

Sometimes popular fishing areas have signs like this posted to remind people of the laws, but not all do.

But before you join the ranks of catfish fishers, make sure you can fish legally in your state. Every U.S. state and Canadian province has its own rules and regulations for fishing its waters, including where and when you can catch certain fish and how much you can catch. You may need a fishing license depending on your age. You can often apply for a license online if you do need one. Check the website of your state or provincial fish and wildlife agency. You can sometimes get a license for just a few days or as long as several years. Since most catfish are freshwater fish, look for a freshwater license. A bonus is that most of the fees for licenses go back into caring for the environment. If you're caught fishing without a license, be prepared to pay a fine.

Some people are into the sport of catfish fishing to break records for the heaviest or longest fish caught. Even young fishers have been in the news for some amazing catches. In 2021, a 13-year-old boy reported catching a 55-pound (25 kg) blue catfish in a lake in New Mexico. In 2022, a 10-year-old reeled in a 70-pound (31.8 kg) flathead off a dock on an Alabama lake. And in 2023, a seven-year-old caught a 105-pound (47.6 kg) blue catfish in a lake in North Carolina. These weren't even record catches! With a bit of luck and some knowledge about these fish and the sport of fishing, you might be the next record breaker in the news.

CHAPTER 1
BE PREPARED

You might think of fishing for catfish as a calm, safe activity. It can be—for those who are prepared. Outdoor activities, especially those around water, call for the proper precautions and preparations. Accidents can happen even for the most experienced fishers. Being mindful of the environment where you'll be fishing is key for safety. Gathering the right gear will also give you confidence before and during your expedition. The first step to a successful catfish fishing expedition begins before you leave home!

DRESS FOR SUCCESS

Fishing can be a messy activity, so dress in clothes that you won't mind getting dirty. Fishing on the shores of a lake or river can mean getting muddy or wet. Standing around all day in wet shoes or sneakers isn't comfortable, so many people who fish choose to wear rubber boots that reach up to their knee or higher. These should have rubber bottoms that prevent slipping.

Be wary about stepping into the water. Catfish often live in rivers with strong currents that can sweep an unsuspecting wader off their feet. If you're knee-deep in the water, stepping into hidden holes or tripping over sunken logs can send you tumbling into a river even if you're inches from the shore.

Whether you're in a boat or on the shore, a hat provides some protection from the sun. It's also a good idea to wear sunblock to prevent sunburn. The light reflecting off the surface of the water increases the chance of a painful sunburn, which can happen even when it isn't summer. You may need to reapply sunblock after a time or if you get wet. The sunblock's directions will tell you how often to do this. In addition, a good pair of polarized sunglasses

BE PREPARED   11

When picking out fishing boots, look for the terms "waterproof rubber" or "water-repellent." If you're fishing from a boat, lower-cut boots may be more comfortable.

will protect your eyes and help you see below the glare of the surface water.

Pack a light raincoat or poncho in case the weather changes. Fishing can often be good during a light rain, but at the first sign of a thunderstorm, it's best to retreat to shelter. Never sit under a tall tree, which can attract lightning. Also, graphite fishing rods can act as lightning rods, so it's best to break them down and wait out a storm in a safe place.

Don't leave home without a good brand of insect repellent. The waterside attracts all sorts of insect pests, including mosquitoes and black flies, which can turn a good fishing day into a miserable experience. Avoid cans of aerosol spray repellents and use roll-on types. They're better for the environment and lighter to carry too.

WOMEN FISH TOO

Did you ever wonder what to call women who fish? So do a lot of people! No, they're not called fisherwomen. Some people use the term "fishers" for both men and women who fish, thinking that "fishermen" means only men who fish. But some women, even those in the commercial fishing industry, prefer to be called fishermen. They say it's not a term for only men. And in fact, many dictionaries define a fisherman as one who fishes, not as a man who fishes.

"Angler" is a term one can use to mean someone who fishes with a rod and line. So, someone who catches fish with a net, for example, wouldn't be an angler. Still, "fishers," meaning people who fish, tends to be used in scientific books and papers. To complicate matters, though, a fisher is also the name for an animal in the weasel family.

BE PREPARED!

In this book, we'll mostly use the term "fishers" or "anglers," but anytime you see the term "fishermen," know that the term includes men and women. After all, women make up about 37 percent of all people who fish, or more than 54 million people, in the United States. They make up about 20 percent of fishers in Canada. But globally, women make up nearly 50 percent of the workers in fisheries.

A record number of women fished in the United States in 2021, according to the Special Report on Fishing by the Recreational Boating and Fishing Foundation.

SAFETY SENSE

Staying safe on a fishing trip means being safe with your equipment and in your environment. You might be focused on the fish, but other animals are around you. Be on the lookout for creatures in the transitional zone between land and water. Remember, this is their home, and they may sense that you are the intruder and respond defensively.

For example, venomous cottonmouth snakes are common throughout freshwater habitats in the U.S. Southeast. They're dangerous only if you stumble on top of them and startle them. Snapping turtles are found in the East. They can be a danger if you enter the water barefoot or attempt to catch and handle one.

Catfish-inhabited water is often best covered by boat, which gives the angler a wider range but also means extra precautions. Always wear a flotation device in a boat and make sure it's securely buckled. Don't go fishing in a canoe or small boat unless accompanied by somebody well trained in handling these often-unstable craft. Never stand up in a small, tippy boat. Kidding around is the number-one cause of accidents on the water. If you do find yourself in the water, your priorities are to save yourself and get onto dry land, not to hold on to your fishing rod.

Your fishing tackle requires some special care to handle it safely. Fishing rods should be transported unassembled and then put together at the fishing spot. Walking through the woods with a fully rigged catfish rod can lead to a broken rod. If you must carry a fully rigged rod through heavy brush, make sure you aren't near any fishing friends who can get poked by the sharp tip of your rod.

A good pocket utility knife has many uses during a fishing trip, whether for opening cans, preparing bait,

BE PREPARED

The cottonmouth snake is sometimes called a water moccasin.

cutting lines, or preparing the catch for dinner. Remember, knives aren't toys. If you're allowed to use one, learn to sharpen it well on a sharpening stone. Most knife accidents occur because a dull blade needs more pressure to cut than a sharp one. Always hand a knife to somebody else with the handle first, and remember to close the blade by folding it between the open palms of your hands—not by holding the blade with your fingers.

Fishhooks for catfish can be small or large, but always handle them with care. The most common mishaps are pricking your finger while tying a knot and snagging a hook on yourself while making a cast. When tying knots or baiting a hook, always be aware of where your line is so that you don't accidentally get yourself or your friend snared in the line with a sharp hook at the end.

FISHING KNOTS

Get to know your fishing knots by practicing at home before you fish. Most fishing lines are made from smooth monofilament nylon, which requires special knots to prevent slipping. The most important knots are the following:

THE IMPROVED CLINCH KNOT
(FOR ATTACHING HOOKS OR LURES TO A LINE)

WHAT TO DO WHEN YOU'RE HOOKED

A first-aid kit is a must for all fishing trips. Include items such as iodine (for disinfecting wounds), bandages, tweezers, and a small wire clipper for cases in which you may have to clip a hook.

If you get a small hook in your finger, the best way to take it out is to grit your teeth, hold the hook by its long shank, and press down to move the bend in the hook into the flesh. This clears the way for the barb to move backward. Then pull it out quickly. Dress the wound with disinfectant and bandage it. You don't want to risk infection by fishing with an open wound. For bigger hooks, it's best to head to the local hospital.

Debarbed hooks (hooks with barbs that have been removed) are easier and safer to remove in case of an accident. They can also be more humane for releasing fish as they're less damaging to them.

A barbless fishhook is good for catch-and-release fishing. A fish can be released from the hook and into the water faster—giving it a better chance at surviving.

THE SURGEON'S KNOT
(FOR ATTACHING TWO PIECES OF LINE TO EACH OTHER)

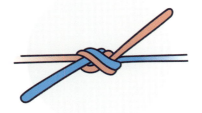

THE DROPPER LOOP
(FOR CREATING A LOOP TO WHICH OTHER RIGS CAN BE TIED)

THE PALOMAR KNOT
(BETTER THAN A CLINCH KNOT FOR HEAVIER, STRONGER LINES)

Being able to tie a knot is an important skill for any fisher. You can practice these to get good at doing them. Online videos can help.

Catfish don't become spooked or wary if they see a heavy fishing line, so if you're going after larger fish or working in water with lots of snags and obstructions, don't be afraid to use a heavier line. Do remember that heavier lines require heavier rods and reels to cast.

Practice your casting without a hook if you haven't been fishing in a while or if you're using a new and unfamiliar rod and reel. Always make sure your fishing friends know when you're about to cast, and—especially when fishing from a cramped boat—be aware of where they are and take care that your cast doesn't come near them.

Tackle accidents often occur when a line becomes snagged in the water and fishers want to retrieve valuable bait or lures. If you fish for catfish, your hook and line will sometimes get caught on rocks or submerged tree trunks. It's almost unavoidable with this kind of fishing. In these cases, don't try to free the line by tugging on the rod—rods can, and do, break. Grabbing a thin monofilament nylon line and tugging at it with your bare hands will guarantee some nasty line cuts too. So, if you do grab the line, protect your hand with a cloth or thick glove. If the snag is serious, accept the loss and cut the line.

There's even some danger once you catch a catfish. More than 1,250 species of catfish are venomous. They have mild venom glands at the base of their pectoral (side) and dorsal (back) spines. When threatened, catfish stiffly extend these spines to prevent predators from eating them. They release venom into the wounds caused by the spines. The danger of getting stung is greatest when landing a catfish or trying to grab a small catfish thrashing in a boat. To avoid a nasty sting, carry an old T-shirt to wrap around the fish when handling it, and take care to avoid the spines. If you do get stung, the greatest danger is from infection: clean the wound with soap and warm water and bandage it. It may hurt like a beesting, but if it swells, don't worry too much: catfish venom is very weak and wears off quickly. Seek professional help if the pain or swelling persists.

CATFISH IN HISTORY

Sure, catfish are an essential part of many ecosystems and a lot of fun to fish. But did you know they're also a part of history? Catfish were an important part of the diets of Native Americans including the Haudenosaunee (Iroquois) of the Northeast, the Secwépemc (Shuswap) of today's British Columbia, the Anishinabe around the Great Lakes, and the Naskapi (Innu) near the St. Lawrence River.

The Anishinabe (also called Ojibwa or Chippewa) had a clan system. Each clan was named for an animal. Catfish was one of the clans. The people in the catfish clan were seen as knowledgeable teachers. They aided children of the clan and helped solve arguments among the clans.

The Menominee of Wisconsin passed down a folktale about how a chief and some catfish worked together to attack a moose. The chief's spear wounded the moose, which then trampled on the heads of the catfish, giving them the flat heads we see today.

According to Japanese myths, Namazu (or Onamazu) was a giant catfish that lived in seas and rivers under the earth. When it swam under the earth's surface, it caused earthquakes. A warrior god named Takemikazuchi-no-mikoto (aka Kashima Daimyojin) placed a stone on the catfish's head to keep it from moving too much, though its slight movements could still cause smaller quakes. (Namazu also brought good fortune to some.)

Japan has experienced many earthquakes throughout its history. The myth of Namazu the giant catfish helped explain these natural occurrences before science could.

CHAPTER 2

GET TO KNOW THE CATFISH

It's good to know a bit about the fish you're going to catch. You need to know some key information, such as where to find them, how large they are, and what they eat. Getting to know the catfish is a bit more of a challenge since it isn't a single species but many. How many? Scientists have identified almost 2,900 catfish species! They're found nearly all over the world. Most live in freshwater environments, but some live in salt water around the tropics. Some are just a few inches (cm) long. Others are longer than 15 feet (4.6 m). Many fishers in North America focus on just a few larger kinds of catfish. These include bullheads, flathead catfish, blue catfish, and channel catfish.

Within their natural ecological systems, large catfish are at the top of the food chain. Once they reach adulthood, they have no enemies besides people and the occasional alligator. They're predators as well as scavengers, constantly on the prowl for food, whether that food is alive or dead. Catfish have broad, shovel-shaped heads, perfect for maintaining balance and control in heavy river currents or for rooting for food on muddy lake bottoms. Catfish lack scales, and their bodies are covered with a protective layer of slimy mucus. Some catfish can even breathe oxygen through their skin and, when faced with drought, walk using their fins from one water source to another!

GET TO KNOW THE CATFISH

The oldest known catfish fossil dates to 70 million years ago. Catfish are survivors!

Catfish barbels are organs that help the fish sense what's around them in their murky surroundings.

CATFISH BEHAVIORS

Every fish species occupies an ecological niche within its aquatic environment. Catfish, however, have evolved to take advantage of a broad range of bodies of water, with each species exhibiting specific preferences and needs. Catfish are especially nocturnal, or active at night, although during the day, they're still alert to any food source and may respond to bait at any time. During the day, catfish usually like to retreat to darker and deeper water. A good fisher can recognize these underwater hiding places and increase their chance of success by casting near them.

Catfish generally like to live in large, slow-moving waters with lots of cover. Small creeks and ponds offer no advantage to a large catfish, although they may be homes to smaller bullheads and channel catfish. Catfish of all sizes like to hide in hollows that give cover and break up flowing currents, such as in sunken trees and behind large rocks. Taking advantage of the current, a catfish usually stays in one place with its head facing upstream to sense food sources flowing downstream toward it. Learning as much as we can about the feeding habits of the fish and its behavior patterns are the keys to fishing success.

A yellow bullhead catfish is shown hiding in a rocky crevice in Florida.

Unlike the males in many other animal species, the male catfish plays a major role in taking care of catfish eggs and young. Catfish spawn when the water warms between late spring and early summer. First, the catfish male and female find a small cave, hollow log, weeds, or another safe place. After the female lays her eggs there, the male fertilizes them. Then the male stays to protect the eggs from hungry fish that would love to dine on catfish eggs. The eggs hatch into baby, or fry, catfish after about 10 days. The father catfish remains on guard until the fry leave the nesting area, about a week later.

SENSING THEIR SURROUNDINGS

Catfish don't have poor eyesight. That's a popular misconception. Their eyes are perfectly suited for the dim and murky water in which they often live. Channel catfish have particularly good vision and are even used by medical centers for research in that field. These catfish, unlike other catfish, may be caught on artificial lures or flies that are attractive only to sharp-sighted fish.

Whatever some catfish lack in vision, they more than make up for with spectacular senses of taste and smell. A catfish is so sensitive to taste that it's like a giant tongue! Catfish have cells much like taste buds all over their body. A 6-inch (15 cm) catfish may have more than 250,000 taste buds on its body. The catfish's barbels are even more densely packed with taste receptors, and they're highly sensitive to vibrations in the water. Taste alerts the catfish to the presence of food—alive or dead—in the water.

Closely related to taste is the catfish's sense of smell. A catfish's nostrils have special folds that alert it to even faint aromas in the water flowing toward it. A channel

GET TO KNOW THE CATFISH

Scientists have discovered that catfish become frightened when they see a shadow, perhaps thinking it's a predator. Avoid casting a shadow over your fishing area.

catfish has 140 folds in its nostrils, while a trout has 18, and a bass only 10. Catfish can sense a meal from far away, and they can also sense strange and unpleasant smells, such as gasoline, insect repellent, and tobacco. So be careful when handling your bait and tackle—the fish will be able to smell you and may become alarmed.

Catfish have a peculiarly acute sense of hearing. All fish have a special system of organs called a lateral line along their body to sense low frequency sounds and vibrations. Catfish, however, also have a swim bladder—an organ that controls a fish's floating ability—that is directly connected to tiny bones in their ears called otoliths. Trout or bass can hear sound vibrations from about 20 to 1,000 cycles per second. Catfish hearing is much more acute, sensing up to 13,000 cycles per second.

Most amazingly, catfish can sense the electric fields given off by living creatures. Their head is covered in tiny cells that act like radar, responding to faint electric signals. This sense, known as electroreception, allows catfish to sense small creatures such as insects and baby fish as they root into the muddy bottom of rivers and lakes. However, it's only effective at close range, just a few centimeters.

MEET THE BULLHEADS

Bullheads (called "horned pout" in some areas of the United States and Canada) are smaller catfish that are rarely larger than 20 inches (51 cm) in length. Bullheads live and feed mostly on the bottoms of lakes, ponds, and slow-flowing rivers and streams. The current world record for the heaviest bullhead according to the International Game Fish Association (IGFA) is 8 pounds 2 ounces (3.69 kg). It was caught in Massapequa Lake, New York, in 2015.

The most common bullhead is the brown bullhead *(Ameiurus nebulosus)*, but the smaller yellow and black bullheads all share similar habits. Technically a bullhead, the white catfish *(Ameiurus catus)* is somewhat larger and behaves more like a channel catfish. Bullheads are tolerant of warm or even heavily polluted water. They prowl the muddy bottom scavenging for food, living or dead. Aquatic insects, crustaceans, dead fish, and plants and algae make up a bullhead's diet. The lessons learned from fishing and catching bullheads help anglers as they move up to fishing for the bullhead's larger cousins.

The brown bullhead is sometimes called a mud cat.

THE BIGGEST CATCHES

Catfish can grow to truly giant sizes. The world record is 646 pounds (293 kg)—and over 9 feet (2.7 m) long—for the Mekong giant catfish of Southeast Asia. This species is now critically endangered, and efforts are underway to breed Mekong catfish to help save the species from extinction. In Europe, the giant wels catfish is a popular food and game fish living in large rivers and lakes. Anglers report catching wels catfish as heavy as 280 pounds (127 kg), but larger fish up to 300 pounds (136 kg) have been reported. The scariest catfish may be the goonch catfish, which lives in cold river waters of South and Southeast Asia. Growing to over 6 feet (1.8 m) in length and weighing upward of 160 pounds (73 kg), the goonch is a greedy feeder. Goonches have even been suspected of attacking and killing swimmers in India.

CHASING THE CHANNEL CATFISH

The channel catfish *(Ictalurus punctatus)* is the single most sought-after game fish of the catfish family in North America. Sleek and strong, the channel catfish averages 2 to 4 pounds (0.9 to 1.8 kg). But the world-record channel catfish, pulled from the Santee-Cooper Reservoir in South Carolina in 1964, weighed 58 pounds (26.3 kg).

Channel catfish like clear, clean water and live in large lakes and flowing rivers. They can also be found in cold water such as trout streams. Channel catfish seek out sheltered areas such as hollow logs and old muskrat holes in which to hide. Channel catfish eat insects, crayfish, plants, and even frogs, but they're more likely to prefer live fish and will chase their prey at great speed. Mostly active at

GET TO KNOW THE CATFISH

Channel catfish can live in salt water but are usually found in fresh water.

night, channel cats often like to lie in the deeper, dimmer depths of a river (thus the name "channel" catfish) during the day.

FIND THE FLATHEAD CATFISH

The flathead *(Pylodictis olivaris)*—sometimes called yellow catfish—are mainly carnivores and grow to weights of over 100 pounds (45 kg). The world record for a flathead catfish catch was 123 pounds (56 kg), caught in 1998 in Elk City Reservoir, Kansas. The flathead is the most nocturnal of all American catfish, feeding mostly at night and preferring live bait.

Like all North American catfish, the flathead lacks sharp teeth and uses its huge mouth to suck unsuspecting fish down into its bony gullet, or throat. Its size and feeding habits make it a target for fishers who like to catch it using only their bare hands in a form of fishing called "noodling."

The tail fin of the flathead catfish isn't as deeply forked as the tail fins of the blue and channel catfish are.

OBSERVING THE BLUE CATFISH

Blue catfish *(Ictalurus furcatus)* are North America's largest catfish. Physically, they resemble the silvery channel cat, but they can grow much larger: the world record, caught in 2022 on the Mississippi River near Natchez, Mississippi, weighed in at 131 pounds (59 kg). To grow that big, the blue catfish is an efficient hunter. It eats larger fish, especially bullheads, and even small animals such as muskrats and baby ducks when it can nab them.

Blue catfish are frequently found in deep areas of large rivers and lakes but also swim in areas with fast currents, where they can catch passing prey—alive or dead—more easily. Some anglers like to pursue this fish because it gives them a good fight on the line!

CATFISH FISHING LIKE A PRO

The blue catfish can live up to 25 years in the wild. That gives it a lot of time to grow to a large size.

A BIT ABOUT WORLD RECORDS

How do anglers and other fishers get credited with world records? Many submit an application to the International Game Fish Association (IGFA). This organization maintains the world records for game fish species. Game fish are those fish that anglers like to try to catch, whether to eat or to release, because of the fish's size and the excitement of reeling them in. The IGFA keeps records of length and weight for both freshwater and saltwater fish as well as records for adult male anglers, adult female anglers, junior anglers (ages 11 to 16), and young anglers (ages 10 and under).

The IGFA has certain rules. For example, the fish must be a recognized species with a scientific name. The IGFA must be able to identify the fish caught based on photographs and other information in the detailed application for the record. And the fish must be considered "trophy size," which means it must be within the top half of the maximum reported weight (or length) for the species. The IGFA suggests anglers check weights and lengths for fish species at www.fishbase.org. The application also asks for information such as where the fish was caught, where it was weighed, other people who saw the fish, how long it took the fish to be reeled in, and data about the rod, reel, line, hooks, and bait used. In fact, the length of the line used must also be submitted to the IGFA. Anglers can also contact state or provincial fish and wildlife agencies to confirm records in those areas.

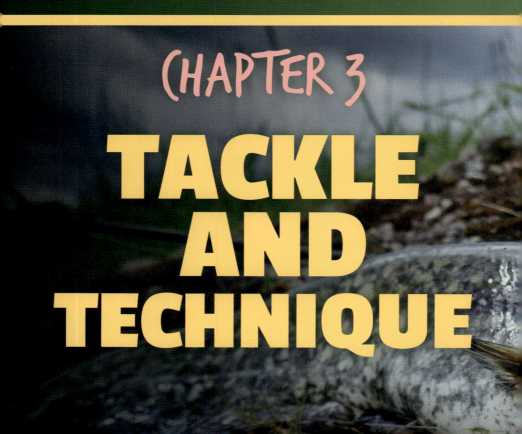

CHAPTER 3
TACKLE AND TECHNIQUE

Now that you know more about the catfish you're pursuing, it's time to get your tackle together. That means rods, reels, lines, and hooks. The right tackle gives an angler a better chance of success. The gear doesn't need to be expensive, but it's important to know what choices are out there.

Every catfish angler will have different preferences about their gear. Some might not want a heavy rod, for example, even though that rod might be better for catching a heavy fish. A good start would be a medium-weight spinning rod and reel. The line is also important. Some experts suggest a monofilament between 12- to 17-pound (5 to 7.7 kg) test for channel catfish. (Test means the amount of weight that can be applied to the line before it breaks.) Stronger lines are needed for blue catfish and flatheads.

THE RIGHT REELS

By far the most popular method for freshwater fishing today is spin fishing. A spinning reel has a fixed, unmovable spool holding the line and a metal bail that's opened before making the cast. The angler pinches the line to the rod with their index finger while making the cast and gracefully brings the rod forward, releasing the line by pointing their finger outward when the rod is pointing at the casting target. When the line hits the water, they close the bail by turning the reel handle.

Like most reels, a good spinning reel should have an adjustable drag. The drag controls how fast the line can be pulled off the spool. When a big fish takes the bait, it should be able to pull some line off the reel or else it may easily break the line. For any fish over 3 pounds (1.4 kg), a good drag is indispensable.

For the largest fish, most experienced catfish anglers choose to use a baitcasting reel and rod. Baitcasting reels sit on top of the rod, and the line is stored on a rolling spool. A crank handle operates the line retrieve. Somewhat trickier to cast, most modern baitcasting reels usually feature a level-wind mechanism, which controls the speed of the line spool to prevent tangling during casts. Larger baitcasting rods are more effective at bringing up large fish from the bottom of rivers with strong currents, making them a favorite of those who target larger flathead and blue catfish.

A baitcasting reel can hold longer lines of heavier monofilament, which are needed to catch larger catfish.

Younger and beginner anglers may choose to use a spincasting rod and reel combo. The advantage is that it's light and easy to use, a compromise between a spinning rod and a light baitcasting rod. Spincasting reels have a cover over the line spool. Instead of using the index finger to control the cast, a simple button or lever is pushed and released. Spincasting is fine for catching smaller catfish such as bullheads and for panfish such as sunfish and perch. But anything larger and the angler will have a hard time bringing the fish in—and may even ruin their reel.

Spincasting reels like this are good for beginners and reduce the possibility of twisting the line.

A BIG, BIG BITE

In May 2023, an Italian professional angler caught what may be the largest catfish by length yet. While fishing in a muddy, flooded section of the Po River in northern Italy, Alessandro Biancardi felt a tug at the end of his rod. He could tell it was something both large and strong. Thus began a mighty struggle between fisherman and catfish. After about 40 minutes of wrestling with the beast, Biancardi got a good look at his foe and realized its enormous size. He found out it was too large to bring in with his rod. So he maneuvered the fish over to the shore and finally got it on land.

He called a friend over to take his picture with the fish. He measured it to be 285 centimeters, or 9.35 feet, which is 4 centimeters longer than the previous world record for a wels catfish as recognized by the IGFA. That fish had been caught by German anglers in April 2023, also in the Po River. Biancardi had 10 witnesses present to verify his story and the catfish's length. He didn't weigh the fish, though. He didn't want to keep it on shore any longer than necessary as that would risk its life. He decided to release it so that it could give "the same joy" to someone else. He sent the measurements and proof to the IGFA to be certified as a new catch-and-release world record.

RESTING THE ROD

Catfish are caught by a variety of other methods other than traditional rods. Fly fishers rarely catch catfish because they rarely use natural bait. But in recent years, more and more have targeted sharp-eyed channel cats with realistic-looking artificial lures, especially those catfish that inhabit the clear tailwaters downstream of reservoir dams.

In places where it's legal, many people set what are called trot lines for catfish. These are lines between trees, poles, or floats that hang over the water, with shorter baited lines that drop down every few feet. They're set out overnight, and fishers check the lines in the morning for any hooked catfish.

Some people keep things even simpler: they catch catfish with their bare hands! This form of fishing has developed into a sport called noodling, or sometimes just handfishing. A team of two people, a spotter and a catcher, dive into the water, feeling around with their hands for the holes and other hiding places that blue catfish and flathead catfish—which like to stay in one place—inhabit. When a catfish is surprised, it clamps down on the noodler's fist. The noodler then wrestles the fish to the surface. It can be dangerous to wrestle a 60-pound (27 kg) fish (or a heavier one) to the surface, but since the fish has no sharp teeth, the noodler usually suffers no more than a bruise.

Noodling has become so popular in some places that the Okie Noodling Festival is held annually at Pauls Valley, Oklahoma. Besides this state, as of 2022, noodling is legal in Alabama, Arkansas, Georgia, Illinois, Kansas, Kentucky, Louisiana, Maryland, Mississippi, North Carolina, South Carolina, Tennessee, Texas, West Virginia, and Wisconsin.

RIGGING FOR BULLHEADS

Bullheads are often the first catfish most beginners catch, and the techniques used will go a long way to preparing them for catching larger catfish. Like most catfish, bullheads feed mostly on the bottom, and they're almost always caught on bait, rarely on artificial lures. The best baits by far are garden worms and the larger worms called night

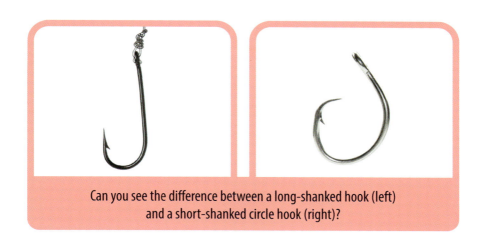

Can you see the difference between a long-shanked hook (left) and a short-shanked circle hook (right)?

crawlers. In June and July, crayfish are a great bullhead bait as well—you can catch them by hanging a piece of chicken neck in the water on a string and carefully pulling it up.

A 6- to 10-pound (2.7 to 4.5 kg) test monofilament line will handle most bullhead catches. Hooks can be relatively large—between size 6 and size 1—and long-shanked, since a bullhead will typically swallow a bait deep, making hook removal difficult. One remedy for this is to use the newly designed, short-shanked circle hooks, which won't hook into a fish's gullet.

A good basic terminal, or end of the line, rig for bullheads is the "slip rig" using a small oval-shaped sliding sinker. Crimp on a small split-shot sinker to the line about 1 foot (30.5 cm) above the hook to prevent the sinker from sliding all the way to the hook. This will allow the bait to rest on the bottom. When a fish takes the bait, it can move with the line without feeling the weight of the heavy sinker. (Many fish will spit out bait prematurely if they feel any weight at all.) Let the fish run with the bait for a few seconds, then take in your slack line and lift the rod to set the hook firmly.

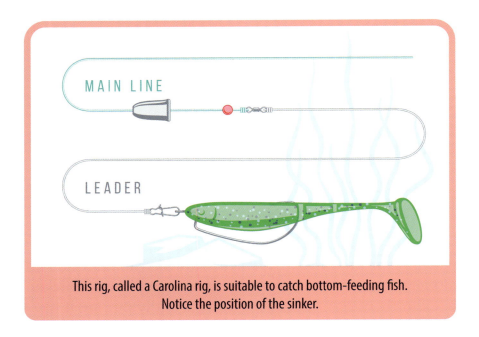

This rig, called a Carolina rig, is suitable to catch bottom-feeding fish. Notice the position of the sinker.

CHASING THE BIG CATS

Channel, blue, and flathead catfish are opportunistic feeders just like bullheads. If targeting larger channel cats, use a medium-weight spinning rod and around a 10-pound (4.5 kg) test line to deal with the kind of snags and obstacles often found in channel catfish waters.

Channel cats will eat almost anything. Once a fish grows to more than 20 inches (51 cm), however, it increasingly depends on live fish for food. While usually seeking out deeper protected areas in the water, catfish can be found in different areas of a lake or river. Learn to read the flow of a river to find the cavernous holes, undercut banks, and deep channels where the fish will lie and where food is easily available. Channel cats, like all larger catfish, are nocturnal, and some of the best catches happen after sundown.

Channel catfish, like bullheads, love big, juicy night crawlers. Minnows fished off a sliding sinker rig will also lure a large catfish, and many veteran anglers swear by cut bait—a hunk of fish cut up and strung on a hook. Cut bait also offers enticing odors for the sensitive catfish to detect.

Aromas attract fish over long distances, and anglers have long sworn by "stink baits." Some are made from liver, chicken guts, fish guts, or chicken blood. Many recipes call for balls of dough flavored by liver, blood, fruit jam, and even vanilla extract. Cheese seems to work well in all mixed stink baits and is a good bet when other baits are passed by. Plain Ivory soap, cut into cubes, is also a favorite stink bait that has been proven to work!

While all the above classic baits will do, blue and flathead catfish are usually sought using live fish up to 1 foot (30.5 cm) in length or larger pieces of cut fish bait on the bottom using a larger and heavier version of the classic slip rig.

Some anglers spend almost as much time catching baitfish as fishing for the catfish itself. Bluegills, sunfish, perch, and especially bullheads fished on large (size 2/0 to 4/0) hooks make good bait for large catfish. Don't expect a lot of fast fishing action when fishing large baits for big fish, though. It can take hours for a big blue or flathead catfish to take an interest in your bait, but when it does, hold on tight! When reeling in a large fish, most anglers use the rod to tire the fish out as it resists capture. By alternately pumping the rod upward to pull the fish toward you and then reeling in the slack line, you can gradually bring the fish to the net. Expect a truly large catfish to put up a fight that can last almost an hour.

48 CATFISH FISHING LIKE A PRO

Some anglers feed line to a nibbling catfish, so it won't get spooked. When the fish takes the line, anglers set the hook, which means making a sudden lifting motion.

FISHING FROM BOATS

When looking for big catfish, many people use boats to get them out to deeper water. They may choose to anchor in one place or let the boat drift if the wind isn't too strong. Special care is needed when fishing in a boat to avoid line tangles and to cast lines safely. Boat fishing for catfish, however, usually means the same bottom-fishing technique that applies to most other forms of catfishing. Catfish don't actively chase fish at the middle levels of a waterway, so trolling (slowly fishing a bait or lure behind a moving boat) is rarely used as a catfishing tactic. Landing a large catfish in a small boat takes special skill, so be really careful when that big fish comes to the surface!

When you're fishing from a boat, remember to wear a life jacket.

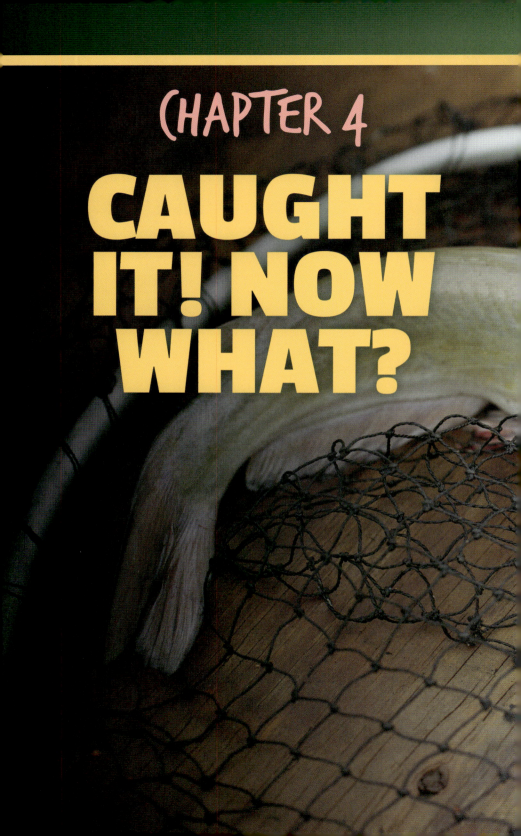

CHAPTER 4
CAUGHT IT! NOW WHAT?

After you catch a catfish, you need to decide—and quickly—whether you want to keep it or throw it back in the water to live another day. Some sport anglers say, "A good game fish is too good to be caught only once." But many people depend on catfish for food. Catfish meat is low in calories and high in protein. It's also a good source of nutrients, including vitamin B12 and omega-3 and omega-6 fatty acids. If you think you'll be doing a lot of catch-and-release, you should use hooks with their barbs crushed down or without barbs and a good hook removal tool so that you can do as little harm to the fish as possible.

Even if you do want to keep some of your catch for dinner, some catfish are better off being released. Catfish from weedy, murky waters often taste muddy, while fish caught in clear or flowing waters taste better. Large catfish aren't as good for eating as smaller catfish: the best catfish for eating are under 10 pounds (4.5 kg). Large catfish are also the ones most likely to have absorbed toxic chemicals into their fat and bones from water pollution, so it may be best to release them to breed another generation.

Whether you're keeping or releasing your fish, you'll need a net to get it up a steep riverbank, into a boat, or onto a dock. Nets for catfish should be long, large, and stout. While many anglers will simply grab a catfish by gripping its lip and jaw in their hands, you can use a special tool called a fish grip to do the same thing without the danger of hurting your hands. When taking the fish from the net or handling it on land or in a boat, take special care to avoid the sharp, venomous spines on its fins and back. Use work gloves, a damp towel, or a thick T-shirt to hold the fish. And be aware that touching a fish's skin can remove the protective mucus on it, making it more vulnerable to infections after release into the water.

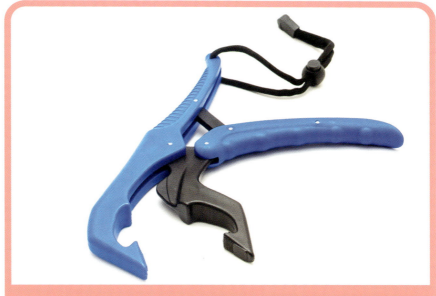

A tool called a fish grip lets anglers grip their fish by its lower jawbone, harming it less than holding its body. Some fish grips even weigh the fish at the same time.

If you decide to keep the fish for food, the fastest and most humane method of killing a catfish is called pithing. This method requires skilled and confident knife skills and should be done only by someone with experience. Place a strong sharp knife directly above the head behind the catfish's two eyes and plunge it into the fish's skull, cutting into the brain. (Take extra care if using a pocketknife that the blade doesn't close.) This quick movement will save the catfish from unnecessary suffering. People once suggested clubbing catfish with a stick, but catfish are tough and clubbing them will often only stun them. When the fish has stopped moving, keep it in a cool place—an ice chest, an insulated fish bag, or even under wet cloth—until you can clean it.

CAPTURE THE MEMORY

So, you've got your fish. Now what? People who have caught a really big fish usually want something to remember it by. The best way to preserve the memory of a good fish is simply to take a photograph of it. If you intend to release your fish unharmed, try to handle the fish as little as possible, and take a photo of it while it's still in the water—there is no need to haul the fish up on dry land and put it through extra stress.

Some fishers take their catch to a taxidermist to be mounted as a trophy fish that can be hung on a wall. This is a somewhat expensive process that requires careful preservation of the fish immediately after catching it. Today, many anglers simply measure their fish, take a photo of it, and send these to a taxidermist who then molds a perfect plastic replica of the fish to hang on the wall.

Whether you catch and release or cook and eat your catch, get a photograph of your fish. Do it quickly to do the least amount of harm to the fish.

CLEANING A CATFISH

Cleaning your catch—removing the inner organs, cleaning out the cavity, and skinning it—is best done as soon as possible, as fish can easily spoil. There isn't just one method of doing this, but here's a popular technique:

Start by cutting the stomach open from the anal vent up toward the gills. Remove the inner organs completely, and discard them. (Or these can be saved for future catfish stink bait.) Rinse the fish and take care to scrape and rinse out the dark, bloody spleen that runs along the top of the body cavity beneath the spine.

To skin a catfish takes skill and practice—and a good pair of pliers. The easiest way to do it is to nail the head of the catfish to a tree or to a wooden board, letting the fish hang down. Cut the skin in a circle around the body just below the head and gills, and with a pair of pliers grab the skin and pull down. It may not all come off in one piece, but soon you'll have a clean white fish ready for filleting.

Small catfish, such as bullheads, may not need to be filleted, but catfish have a delicate white flesh and a strong bone structure that makes filleting easy. You can use a filleting knife with a long, thin, sharp blade, but any good knife will work. Place the fish on its side and make two slices alongside the dorsal fin that runs along the back of the fish. With a pair of pliers, you can now pull the dorsal fin completely out. Now run your knife alongside the body of the fish until it reaches the bones of the spine. Flatten your knife angle and slice carefully next to the bone, freeing the flesh from the ribs to the fatty area of the stomach. Use short slicing cuts until you have smooth, boneless catfish fillets. You can freeze your fillets in sealable plastic bags—

catfish keep well in the freezer—or you can try any of the many traditional recipes for which catfish are famous.

CATFISH FILLETS

The classic way of preparing catfish in some places, especially the American South, is to roll the fish in cornmeal or crushed crackers and fry it in melted lard, bacon fat, or vegetable oil. Try this recipe. Be very careful when placing the fish in the hot oil.

INGREDIENTS

- 1 cup cornmeal
- ½ teaspoon pepper
- ½ teaspoon salt
- vegetable oil for frying
- 4 catfish fillets

DIRECTIONS

1. In a large skillet or frying pan, heat ½ inch of oil over medium-high heat.
2. Place the cornmeal in a bowl. Add salt and pepper, and stir.
3. Coat each fillet with the mixture on both sides.
4. Turn the stove heat down to medium. Place each fillet in the oil and cook, turning once, until browned on both sides, about four minutes.
5. Remove the fish carefully and place it on a plate covered with a paper towel.
6. Serve fillets with lemon wedges, vinegar, tartar sauce, or the southern favorite for catfish, ketchup.

Clean tasting, firm, and healthy, catfish fillets are perfect for people who prefer fish that doesn't smell or taste "too fishy."

CATFISH DISHES AROUND THE WORLD

Catfish is the sixth most popular seafood in the United States. In 1987, President Ronald Reagan declared June 25 as National Catfish Day to celebrate farm-raised catfish. This fish is also popular in Canada and other nations around the world too.

In the South American country of Columbia, catfish is sometimes fried or grilled whole and served with plantains or yucca (or cassava). In Nigeria in West Africa, catfish is often simmered with crushed pumpkin seeds to make spicy egusi soup. In Hungary in Eastern Europe,

Egusi soup, a West African traditional dish, makes use of whatever fish or meat is available. Catfish is a tasty possibility.

it's stewed in paprika sauce and served over flat noodles as harcsapaprikás. In Thailand, catfish is eaten fried or in curries, and soup.

The world-record catfish—the whopping 646-pound (293 kg), 9-foot-long (2.7 m) Mekong giant catfish caught in Thailand in May 2005—was eaten. While waiting for scientists to retrieve the giant fish, the villagers decided the fish would spoil, so they cut it into steaks for food.

Catfish, like most freshwater fish, should never be eaten raw due to the presence of microscopic parasites that can make people ill. These are destroyed by the heat of the cooking process, but never experiment with catfish sushi or serve undercooked freshwater fish.

CATFISH FARMS

Not everyone needs to catch their own fish to eat. Some just go to the store. Aquaculture is the breeding, raising, and harvesting of fish, shellfish, and water plants. It's a big business in the United States and Canada. According to the U.S. Department of Commerce's National Oceanic and Atmospheric Administration (NOAA), almost half the fish people eat around the world is raised in fish farms. Catfish aquaculture is the largest aquaculture industry in the United States, with reported sales of $421 million in 2021. The most commonly raised catfish is the channel catfish, which makes up about 90 percent of farm-raised catfish. Blue catfish, which have more meat but take longer to grow, are also a popular fish to farm.

In the United States, most catfish farms are in the Southeast, particularly in Mississippi where more than 50 percent of farm-raised catfish come from. A catfish farm isn't the kind of farm where crops such as corn and wheat grow. Instead, it has many freshwater ponds, often lined with clay. Most ponds are between 4 and 6 feet (1.2 to 1.8 m) deep and as wide as 20 acres (8 ha).

Catfish in these large ponds are given special foods in the form of pellets, often mostly made of soybean. When the catfish spawn, the eggs are taken to hatcheries. Later, young catfish, or fingerlings, are then taken to another pond until they grow larger. Catfish are raised about two years, or until they're about 1.7 pounds (770 g). Then they're taken out of the ponds using nets, loaded onto a truck, and transported to a processing facility where they're prepared for stores.

While aquaculture might sound like it's the ideal way to raise fish for food, there are drawbacks to the way fish are

About 94 percent of U.S. farm-raised catfish comes from Alabama, Arkansas, Louisiana, and Mississippi.

raised on some farms. For example, farms for saltwater fish are placed in pens in marine waters. If the farmed fish get a disease, it spreads quickly in their tightly packed cages. And it can then spread to wild fish that are swimming by. In addition, some farmed fish escape to become invasive predators of native fish. On inland farms for freshwater fish, parasites and disease can spread quickly too, especially if the water quality becomes poor. Also, fish fecal matter and fish food can pollute waterways. Still, fish farming is here to stay, so people are looking for ways to improve the processes involved.

CHAPTER 5

CATFISH AND NATURE

Most people who spend a lot of time in nature, as fishers do, realize what precious natural resources lakes, rivers, and streams are as well as the creatures that live in them. They may see how climate change and pollution affect the plants and animals of their favorite fishing spots. They may recognize how a change to one plant or animal can make waves throughout a habitat. They hopefully also recognize the responsibility that each angler has to keep the environment as pristine as possible. They can speak out to the wider community so that others realize the great effects that people's actions can have on nature.

As cities and industries expand and grow, wild and productive habitats need to be protected from destruction by pollution, overdevelopment, and environmental accidents. Fish and the water that they inhabit aren't inexhaustible resources. The Mekong giant catfish in Southeast Asia—the world's largest catfish—is critically endangered, prevented from reaching its breeding grounds by dams built to provide power and flood control for the growing number of people living along the rivers. Sometimes, the needs of people and the needs of fish don't go hand in hand. Difficult decisions must be made.

Many fish that we depend on for food are in danger of possible extinction unless better fishing regulations can be agreed upon by the many different nations that fish for them. North America has seen the gradual disappearance of commercial fisheries such as that of the migratory Atlantic salmon, blocked by river dams from its breeding grounds. The once rich cod fisheries off the Grand Banks of Newfoundland collapsed in the 1990s due to overfishing caused by modern fishing nets replacing the older technique of line fishing. Both sport and commercial fishers, who are always

Dams like this one in China disrupt the life cycle of migratory fish such as the Mekong giant catfish.

the first to notice changes in fish populations, are among the most organized and vocal environmental activists.

Many kinds of catfish, however, have adapted and evolved to the top of the food chain in a wide range of aquatic environments. Most catfish species in North America are not in danger of being overfished, even with the increasing popularity of freshwater fishing as a hobby. In fact, by targeting certain catfish species, anglers take the pressure off fish species such as bass and trout that can easily be overfished by sport anglers. Many lake-fishing organizations encourage fishing for bullheads, which hungrily target the eggs of other game fish species and can easily take over a small bass or panfish pond.

CLEAN WATER ONLY

Many kinds of catfish, especially bullheads, are surprisingly tolerant of living in water that's more polluted than most other fish species can tolerate. They can often be found living in rivers that flow through built-up cities and in country farm ponds that may be full of chemical fertilizers from agriculture. While common bullheads are able to survive in polluted water, they accumulate the pollutants in their bodies. Therefore, in some waters, bullheads contain higher levels of contaminants. Larger, older fish—over 20 pounds (9 kg)—are even more at risk from contaminants such as heavy metals and PCBs that collect on the silt of lake and river bottoms. Always check first to see if it's safe to consume your catch from a body of water, whether it looks polluted or not. Your local or state fish and wildlife agency will often have a free pamphlet or a list on its website citing warnings about polluted waters.

One kind of pollution fish encounter is runoff from farms that use chemical fertilizers. When rainwater drains from farmlands, it takes fertilizers with it.

CATFISH AND NATURE

CONTRIBUTE TO THE CLEANUP

Fishing is a sport that requires an awareness of the natural environments that fish and wildlife need to flourish. Since a fisher depends on the health of the natural environment to provide access to healthy fish and fun sport, everyone should do as much as possible to maintain pollution-free forests and clean waters. Always try to leave the woods or riverbanks with whatever you carried in with you. Bait boxes, soda cans, sandwich wrappers . . . leave nothing behind but your footprints. Carry a garbage bag with you and try to collect any discarded fishing line or trash that other, less respectful, anglers may have left behind.

Much of the catfish we eat comes from catfish farms with clean rock, clay, or gravel ponds adapted to catfish farming. Many offer recreational fishing for a small fee, often renting out rods and charging on a per-pound basis for any fish caught. This may not seem like the most sporting method of fishing, but it does guarantee a clean catch and has virtually no negative impact on the environment. And it's a great activity for friends and family!

INVASIVE CATFISH

Some catfish species are released into bodies of water where they are not native. When they do ecological harm to the habitats, they're called invasive species. Some invasive catfish endanger other catfish species as well as other kinds of fish. This has happened in many areas of the United States and Canada. For example, in the Yadkin River of North Carolina, the populations of the catfish called snail bullheads and flat bullheads declined sharply after the introduction of nonnative flathead catfish, which eat bullheads and compete for food sources. It's possible that fishers introduced the flathead to the waters because these catfish grow larger than bullheads, but the fishers didn't recognize the dangers to other creatures in the habitat. Once a species is introduced, it's very hard to remove it.

In another North Carolina body of water, Salem Lake, a truck that brought in fingerling channel catfish to stock the lake mistakenly introduced a small number of fingerling flatheads in the 1970s. Today, flatheads thrive in the lake, sometimes eating the popular largemouth bass that many anglers fish for there.

WALKING NIGHTMARE

Natural ecology is a delicate balance of species that develops over many years. When humans introduce a new species into the mix, it can lead to ecological nightmares. In the 1960s, the walking catfish, an aquarium fish imported from Thailand, escaped from tropical fish breeding farms in Florida. As long as its skin remains moist, the catfish can "walk" using its fins between different bodies of water, feeding on native fish. Wild walking catfish can carry a disease that can affect other native species. The disease they carry is called enteric septicemia, which is caused by a bacterium. In 1967, Florida banned importing and even owning these catfish. It's believed that this measure caused breeders and owners to release even more of the catfish into the wild because they didn't want to be caught with them. The owners of fisheries in areas of Florida that are affected by walking catfish often build special fences to keep walking catfish from entering their ponds and spreading the disease to farm-raised fish.

Aquarium dumping—getting rid of aquarium fish by releasing them into the wild—and accidental releases are still a problem, but fishers can help. They can learn about invasive species. If they spot them, they can report them to a local, state, or provincial fish and wildlife agency. Another "must" is to fish with native bait, or bait that is found in or near the waters where they're fishing. When they buy bait from licensed dealers, this isn't usually a problem, but it's best to do research about native bait that will lure the desired fish. Sometimes, anglers dump their nonnative live bait after a day of fishing, contributing to the problem of invasive species.

The silver carp of eastern Asia was introduced to the United States in the 1970s to eat algae growth in wastewater treatment facilities and fish farms. By the 1990s, they had escaped into the Mississippi River and are now considered invasive.

An angler alerted officials in Canada to the presence of black bullheads in a pond in Alberta in 2015. The officials immediately closed the pond to try to capture and kill the invasive fish, knowing how much damage it could do to native species.

Besides disrupting the ecological balance of these waters, invasive catfish can make it tricky for anglers to catch their fish of choice. Anglers must choose which fish to try to catch and adjust their strategy—and bait and tackle—based on that. Plus, those who are trying to reel in a gentle fish won't be expecting the fight that a large catfish will give them!

JOIN THE CLUB

The future of fishing depends on the fishers of the future. Joining a local fishing club is a great way to get tips on hot fishing spots and effective techniques, like how to rig your baits for big catfish. But many fishing clubs also have an eye on the environment. They sponsor annual cleanups of rivers and lakes, sometimes helping rehabilitate aquatic habitats in degraded rivers and lakes for better fishing. Local fishing

CATFISH AND NATURE

Fishing clubs are a great place to learn and make new friends.

clubs connect with larger environmental associations that lobby, or try to influence, governments for better laws to protect waters from pollution and destructive development. Fishing is one of the most popular outdoor activities, and few politicians are willing to ignore the power of votes cast by concerned anglers.

Many fishing clubs work hand in hand with local fish and wildlife agencies, reporting on fish populations, helping with stocking, and informing about violations of fishing regulations they may observe. The fees that come from buying a fishing license go to much more than merely providing stocked fish for anglers to catch. They go to studying and improving the environment. For example, fish and wildlife departments hire environmental researchers to visit bodies of water to test the waters. They may also make counts to see how many fish live in an area. These are often done using an electric shocker that stuns fish but does not kill them. The stunned fish float to the surface where they can be counted, but after a short time, they recover and swim away, leaving the scientists with a census of the fish population and an idea of how healthy a body of water actually is.

In the end, fishing isn't just about catching fish—fishing is about getting to know the fish. As fishing skills develop, you become aware of the world at the end of the fishing line, a world much different from the world up here on dry land. You start to understand a species as different from you as if it came from an alien planet. The more you learn, the more you'll develop a respect for the fish, its behavior, and its environment. It wants something to eat—at a certain time of the year, at a certain time of day, and at a certain place in the water.

As you fish, you'll develop what some fishers call "fish sense." At some point in your fishing career, you'll get a hunch to cast a line in the water and be rewarded with an almost electric jolt as your rod comes to life. With a quick jerk, you'll see a big catfish at the end of the line. You'll be rewarded with the feeling that every angler is chasing and experience the thrill of the sport.

GLOSSARY

acute: Very sensitive or highly developed.
census: An official process of counting.
contaminant: A substance, usually a chemical, found in an environment where it does not belong.
ecological: Concerning the study of the relationships between living organisms and their surroundings.
fillet: To cut slices of meat from a fish's sides so that there are no bones, or those slices of meat.
frequency: How many times a sound wave is repeated during a time period. A low-frequency sound wave creates a low-pitched sound. A high-frequency one creates a high-pitched sound.
graphite: A kind of material in which carbon fibers are the reinforcing matter.
heavy metal: A kind of element found in nature that can become poisonous when absorbed by organisms.
misconception: A mistaken idea.
monofilament: A type of fishing line made from a single, untwisted strand of material, often nylon.
niche: The role or place of an organism in a community.
PCBs: Short for polychlorinated biphenyls, these are highly toxic chemical pollutants once commonly manufactured but now banned.
rehabilitate: To restore something to its original state of health or purity.
rig: Tackle fitted for a certain purpose.
scavenger: An animal that feeds on dead organic matter, often other animals.
spawn: To lay eggs in water.
tackle: The gear or equipment needed for an activity.
taxidermist: One who prepares and preserves the skins of animals for stuffing and mounting them in lifelike form.

For Further Reading

Doyle, Abby Badach. *Freshwater Fishing*. Buffalo, NY: Gareth Stevens Publishing, 2023.

Hamilton, Sue L. *Catfish*. Minneapolis, MN: A&D Xtreme, 2015.

Hogan, Zeb, and Stefan Lovgren. *Chasing Giants: In Search of the World's Largest Freshwater Fish*. Reno, NV: University of Nevada Press, 2023.

Koestler-Grack, Rachel A. *Curious About Freshwater Fishing*. Mankato, MN: Amicus Learning, 2024.

Mazzarella, Kerri. *Freshwater Fishing*. New York, NY: Crabtree Publishing Company, 2023.

Reeves, Diane Lindsey. *Freshwater Fishing*. Minneapolis, MN: Lerner Publications, 2024.

Underwood, Lamar, ed. *1001 Fishing Tips: The Ultimate Guide to Finding and Catching More and Bigger Fish*. New York, NY: Skyhorse Publishing, 2022.

Werner, Robert G. *Freshwater Fishes of the Northeastern United States: A Field Guide*. Syracuse, NY: Syracuse University Press, 2023.

Willis, John. *Freshwater Fishing*. New York, NY: AV2, 2021.

FOR MORE INFORMATION

American Catfish Association (ACA)
P.O. Box 7492
Jupiter, FL 33468
(833) 4.CATFISH (833.422.8347)
email: info@acafishing.com
website: tm.americancatfishingassociation.com
Twitter: @ACAFishing
Facebook: /AmericanCatfishingAssociation/
The ACA offers its members many resources about the sport, the fish, and ACA tournaments.

Association of Fish and Wildlife Agencies
1100 First Street NE, Suite 825
Washington, DC 20002
(202) 838-3474
email: info@fishwildlife.org
website: www.fishwildlife.org
Twitter: @fishwildlife
Facebook: /FishWildlifeAgencies/
The Association of Fish & Wildlife Agencies represents North America's fish and wildlife in Washington, D.C., especially in matters of management and conservation of wildlife and habitats.

The International Game Fish Association (IGFA)
300 Gulf Stream Way
Dania Beach, FL 33004
(954) 927-2628
email: hq@igfa.org
website: www.igfa.org
Twitter: @TheIGFA
Facebook: /International-Game-Fish-Association/
The IGFA is the worldwide authority on sport fishing, including ethical angling practices. It also keeps the world records of game fishing.

The National Wildlife Federation (NWF)
P.O. Box 1583
Merrifield, VA 22116
(800) 822-9919
email: friends@nwf.org
website: www.nwf.org
Twitter: @NWF
Facebook: /NationalWildlife/
Read about the impact this organization has on U.S. wildlife conservation efforts and how it tries to get younger people involved.

Okie Noodling Festival
P.O. Box 638
Pauls Valley, OK 73075
(405) 238-6491
email: president@paulsvalleychamber.COM
website: www.okienoodling.com
Twitter: @noodlepv
Facebook: /okienoodlingfest/
Find out more about this unique competition and sport.

U.S. Fish and Wildlife Service
1849 C Street NW
Washington, D.C. 20240
(800) 344-WILD (1-800-344-9453)
website: www.fws.gov
Twitter: @USFWS
Facebook: /USFWS/
The U.S. Fish and Wildlife Service is the agency in the federal government responsible for the management and conservation of fish, wildlife, plants, and habitats.

INDEX

A
Alabama, 7, 44, 60
aquarium dumping, 69
Arkansas, 44, 60

B
bait, 4, 14, 16, 19, 26, 30, 34, 37, 40, 43, 44, 45, 47, 49, 55, 67, 69, 70
barbels, 4, 26, 28
behaviors, 26, 27, 72
blue catfish, 7, 24, 34, 35, 36, 40, 41, 44, 46, 47, 59
boats, 10, 11, 14, 19, 49, 52
bullheads, 5, 24, 27, 30, 31, 35, 42, 44, 45, 46, 47, 55, 65, 66, 67, 68, 70

C
Canada, 7, 13, 30, 57, 59, 67, 70
catch-and-release fishing, 4, 17, 37, 43, 52, 54
channel catfish, 24, 27, 28, 31, 32, 33, 34, 35, 40, 43, 46, 47, 59, 68
China, 65
cleaning the fish, 53, 55

D
dams, 43, 64, 65
dishes (meals), 57, 58

E
electroreception, 30
eyesight, 28

F
farms, 59, 61, 66, 67, 68, 69
flathead catfish, 5, 7, 24, 34, 40, 41, 44, 46, 47, 68
Florida, 27, 68
fossils, 25
fresh water, 4, 7, 14, 24, 33, 37, 40, 58, 59, 61, 65

G
Georgia, 44

H
heaviest, 7, 30
hooks, 4, 16, 17, 19, 37, 40, 44, 45, 47, 48, 52

I
Illinois, 44
International Game Fish Association (IGFA), 30, 37, 43

J
Japanese catfish myths, 20

K
Kansas, 34, 44
Kentucky, 44
knots, 16, 18

L
largest, 35, 43, 64
licenses, 7, 72

lines, 4, 12, 16, 18, 19, 35, 37, 40, 41, 42, 44, 45, 46, 47, 48, 49, 67, 72, 73
Louisiana, 44, 60
lures, 16, 19, 28, 43, 44, 47, 49

M

Maryland, 44
Mekong giant catfish, 32, 58, 64, 65
Mississippi, 35, 44, 59, 60

N

Native Americans, 20
noodling, 4, 34, 44
North Carolina, 7, 44, 67, 68

O

Okie Noodling Festival, 44
Oklahoma, 44

P

pithing, 53
pollution, 31, 52, 61, 64, 66, 67, 72

R

records, 5, 7, 30, 32, 34, 35, 37, 43, 58
reels, 4, 19, 37, 40, 41, 42, 47
regulations, 7, 64, 72
rigs, 14, 18, 44, 45, 46, 47, 70
rods, 4, 12, 14, 19, 37, 40, 41, 42, 43, 45, 46, 47, 67, 73

S

safety, 10, 12, 14, 49, 66
salt water, 24, 33, 37, 61
sense of hearing, 39
sense of smell, 28, 30
sense of taste, 28
South Carolina, 32, 44
swim bladder, 30

T

Tennessee, 44
Texas, 44

V

venom, 19, 20, 52

W

walking catfish, 68
West Virginia, 44
Wisconsin, 20, 44
women fishers, 12, 13

About the Author

Marie Roesser has been an angler since she was "knee-high to a grasshopper." A lover of all things nature, she's the catch-and-release champion of her local saltwater fishing club and the secretary of her town's conservation society. When not on the water, Roesser can be found in her garden or on her bike. She lives in East Sandwich, Massachusetts.

About the Consultant

Contributor Benjamin Cowan has more than 20 years of both freshwater and saltwater angling experience. In addition to being an avid outdoorsman, Cowan is a member of many conservation organizations. He currently resides in western Tennessee.

Photo Credits

Cover, pp. 22-23 Kletr/Shutterstock.com; pp. 4-7 (background) Kichigin/Shutterstock.com; p. 5 FedBul/Shutterstock.com; p. 6 Arne Beruldsen/Shutterstock.com; pp. 8-9 Dmitry Kalinovsky/Shutterstock.com; p. 11 Volodymyr Tverdokhlib/Shutterstock.com; p. 13 Gerhard Pettersson/Shutterstock.com; p. 15 jo Crebbin/Shutterstock.com; pp. 16, 18 VectorMine/Shutterstock.com; p. 17 Bartlomiej Kaminski/Shutterstock.com; p. 21 https://commons.wikimedia.org/wiki/File:Namazu-e.jpg; p. 25 John Cancalosi/Alamy Stock Photo; p. 26 Martin Prochazkacz/Shutterstock.com; p. 27 Erin Westgate/iStock; p. 29 Fabian Glantschnig/Shutterstock.com; p. 31 Rostislav Stefanek/Shutterstock.com; p. 33 Brookieland/Shutterstock.com; pp. 34-35 Rob Hainer/Shutterstock.com; p. 36 https://commons.wikimedia.org/wiki/File:A_Blue_Catfish_%285794304908%29.jpg; pp. 38-39 wwwarjag/Shutterstock.com; p. 41 Proshkin Aleksandr/Shutterstock.com; p. 42 Dewitt/Shutterstock.com; p. 45 (left) New Africa/Shutterstock.com; p. 45 (right) immfocus studio/Shutterstock.com; p. 46 KrakenRoll/Shutterstock.com; p. 48 LightField Studios/Shutterstock.com; p. 49 Hero Images Inc/Shutterstock.com; pp. 50-51 Jennifer White Maxwell/Shutterstock.com; p. 53 Trong Nguyen/Shutterstock.com; p. 54 M Huston/Shutterstock.com; p. 57 Elena Veselova/Shutterstock.com; p. 58 bonchan/Shutterstock.com; p. 60 Surachet Jo/Shutterstock.com; pp. 62-63 Michael Warwick/Shutterstock.com; p. 65 HelloRF Zcool/Shutterstock.com; p. 66 olpo/Shutterstock.com; p. 69 SandmanPhotography/Shutterstock.com; p. 71 Anatol Tyshkevich/Shutterstock.com.